SHOWERED BY STARLIGHT

OSCILLATING BETWEEN THE PAST AND THE FUTURE

T ABRAHAM

Copyright © T ABRAHAM
All Rights Reserved.

This book has been self-published with all reasonable efforts taken to make the material error-free by the author. No part of this book shall be used, reproduced in any manner whatsoever without written permission from the author, except in the case of brief quotations embodied in critical articles and reviews.

The Author of this book is solely responsible and liable for its content including but not limited to the views, representations, descriptions, statements, information, opinions and references ["Content"]. The Content of this book shall not constitute or be construed or deemed to reflect the opinion or expression of the Publisher or Editor. Neither the Publisher nor Editor endorse or approve the Content of this book or guarantee the reliability, accuracy or completeness of the Content published herein and do not make any representations or warranties of any kind, express or implied, including but not limited to the implied warranties of merchantability, fitness for a particular purpose. The Publisher and Editor shall not be liable whatsoever for any errors, omissions, whether such errors or omissions result from negligence, accident, or any other cause or claims for loss or damages of any kind, including without limitation, indirect or consequential loss or damage arising out of use, inability to use, or about the reliability, accuracy or sufficiency of the information contained in this book.

Made with ♥ on the Notion Press Platform
www.notionpress.com

Contents

Contents

Contents

Credits

All the images used in this book are created with the help of the Artificial Intelligence technology available in the Canva.

Preface

Our minds are functional with the thoughts and ideas being spontaneously produced within it. Our thoughts and actions are majorly being governed by what we see, hear and feel through our senses in our immediate environment. So, what we see and hear from others are something that makes us either an asset or a liable. At times our opinions are without any true premise and we are inside a world of deception were the target entity for everybody is just ourselves. It is said that, 'We cannot come to conclusion about anything by just what we hear and see, but we ourselves should investigate to find out the truth and nature of everything'. So, we are going to look into some of the contaminants that usually contaminate our minds and results in a diseased opinion and how one can avoid this tragedy from happening in one's life.

Firstly, many of us go with what we see. The sight is something which is used by any deceiver to deceive anybody. One's actions paves way for our thoughts to connect, disconnect and reconnect and waver away from our opinions. Many-a-times we are forming opinions by what we perceive about others and it stands true. Doubting the premise formed on first sight is something that is going to cause damage to us and our loved ones. It is rightly said, 'First impression is the best impression'. Getting an impression, that is, a positive or a negative one is often being confused or deliberately being interchanged with being judgemental which is totally wrong.

The one's who can differentiate the deception by sight is blessed with a good understanding of the human nature. But people of the present times are more often interested in ruining other people's nature and happiness these days and are discouraging them by saying they are either being judgemental or unfriendly or unsociable which is totally a technique used to make them think they have formed a false premise. If one falls into this it is referred to as 'falling by words'. This includes the major contaminants namely rumors, gossip, fake news, exaggeration, misunderstanding, etc.,. This technique is used by the deceivers to bring in the feeling of guilt and discomfort for the entity to be ruined and exploited by deception. But if one does not go by these two things and knows the nature of the situation and other humans he is safe from these feelings arising in his mind.

Being introverted, following ones morality, religion and ethics seriously is not a crime and one is always a target for deception by many. Going along on our own way and paths is something that becomes difficult nowadays and we cannot do this without rebellion. One has to understand the cause of his rebellion and if it is for something good, he should not turn back not even once if he is right. Surpassing the deception through sight and words are necessary for one to wholeheartedly find one's passion and interest and to follow it amidst all the ruinsome situations that arises during the journey to one's dream destiny.

T ABRAHAM

CHENNAI, 2024.

Acknowledgements

I would like to thank Dr S. Samuel Rufus sir for encouraging me to identify the dormant poet inside me. I would like to thank sir for constantly motivating me throughout the completion of the 50 poems and for reading the manuscript for finalizing it for publishing. I would also like to thank Dr Mekala Rajan ma'am, Former Head of the Department of English (Aided), Madras Christian College (Autonomous) for motivating me to start writing poems which made me pen down my first three poems which instantly got elevated and has resulted in completion of 200 poems in which my first 50 poems were published as a book titled 'I ADMIRE YOU - A SELF-ADMIRATION OF MY INNER FEELINGS' and my next set of 50 poems were published as a book titled 'Loud Inner Voice: Multiple voices ringing inside' and my next set of 50 poems were published as a book titled 'Sweetness In Nostalgia: Cherishing the past and living the present' and this book contains the poems written after the publication of my third book. I would like to thank Mr J. Arun Kumar sir for being a constant support throughout the writing of this book.

I would like to thank Dr. S. Franklin Daniel sir, Head of the Department and the Department of English (Aided), Madras Christian College (Autonomous) for equipping me with this wonderful art of writing poetry which has resulted in the creation of my fourth book titled 'SHOWERED BY STARLIGHT'.

Last but not the least, I would like to thank my mother and my friends for being a constant support which made me complete writing this book within a limited time frame.

1. The Broken Glass

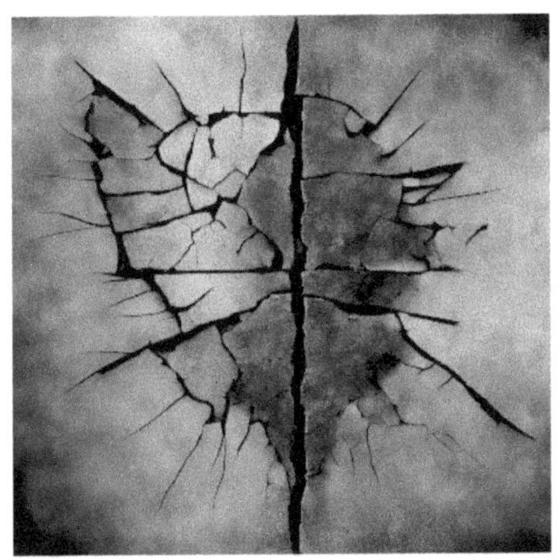

Transparency is maintained,
Pure transparency contained,
Anything can pass through,
My vision and mission is clear,
All the fog and smog may hinder,
You are the truth but fragile,
Your brokenness is so fatal,
None can touch you,
A trust and truth broken,
Pierces every man trying to mend,
But nobody can mend you back,
You make everyone suffer,

If I mend you I bleed,
Bleeding just from the contact,
I cannot touch your brokenness,
You are lost forever more.

2. Sickness In Idleness

Sourness in my tongue,
Heaviness in my lung,
A bitterness in my mouth,
An unknown fatigue,
Unknown dryness on my lips,
No productive nature,
Time passing away,
Unproductive mind,
Conscience is pierced,
No sleep to calm down,
In emptiness, no peace,

Idleness is an unease.

3. The Bearable

The discomfort in new places,
Unknown and new faces,
I am a foreigner in this land,
It is tolerable and I can.
The mocking voices,
And wavering choices,
The bullies and giggles,
It is bearable and I can.
The false claim,
Insult of my name,
An unwavering gossip,
It is unbearable but I can.

The disrespect and abuse,
A tiresome disrepute,
None to turn for comfort,
I am leaving forever.
The bearable is no more,
It is unbearable for ever more.

4. Showered By Starlight

The light falling upon,
Sprinkled everyday,
Reflected lights falling,
Peaceful voices calling,
Stars of comfort falling,
The first of my breath,
Life blood protected,
It was the day of life,
The day of birth and love,
Hugs of comforts given,
It's origin traced backwards,

Moved forward to nineteen,
Likes and dislikes arising,
Voices at times raising,
But never is the supply ceased,
Until the last breath,
It is unleashed.

5. Broken Mind

Confusion confusing one,
Decision taken by someone,
Focus is disappearing,
Fog is appearing,
Nothing to interest,
Nobody to trust,
Anger roaring and raging,
The thunder roaring inside,
It's raining outside,
Roads flooded with impatience,
No signs for pure patience,

Days to live,
Becoming days to drag,
The unhappiness filling,
Conscience smiling.

6. Innocent Smiles

The very presence,
It always makes sense,
With it's essence.

• 12 •

7. Actions and Reactions

Equal cause, unequal loss,
Pause for a moment,
Reactions for an ill comment,
Rotten actions are never pleasant,
Reaction of the mind is ever present,
Never react, response is sensible,
Calmness inside a responding mind,
Avoiding conflict, always so kind,
Reacting and reactions rapidly pouring,
Stopping, pausing and controlling,
Responding more and reacting no more.

8. Being Insensitive

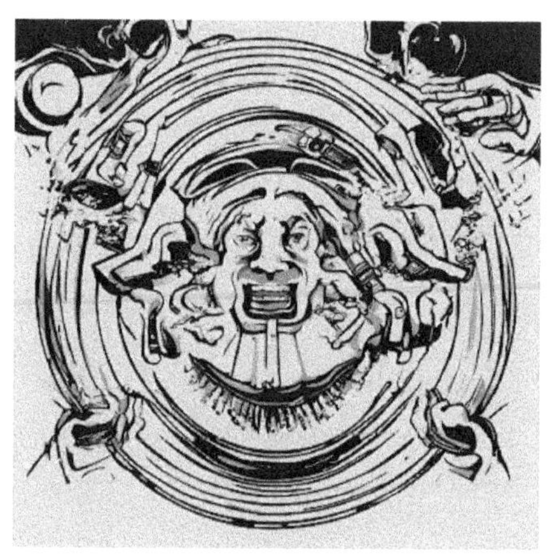

To sensitize or not to?
At times have to be intact,
My heart turns to stone,
At most wants to be alone,
Eating a watermelon,
Taking blood in gallon,
Sensitivity is draining,
Fatigue controlling,
Unhappiness conquering,
Insensitivity is a best help,
A helping hand at dark times.

9. The Rabbit

Sparkling eyes of shyness,
Purity in fur by whiteness,
Your presence is never heard,
A portrayal of gentleness,
Painted with politeness,
In silence is your presence,
But your absence is felt,
A good listener you are,
In danger you live everyday,
Jealousy has poisoned the minds,
Either be a prey or betray,

Protection is a rapid act,
Your life is in simplicity,
But you look gorgeous,
You are robed with beauty,
Beauty inside you is seen,
An everlasting charm in beauty.

10. Words By Herds

The age of courage on a rage,
I follow none for a discourage,
Words, words and words are heard,
These are just mere words spoken by a herd,
Essence felt in some words,
Not mere words from people,
Mere words from a crowd,
Words from the heart is heard,
Only a few can give you this essence,
All others are words by herds.

11. Changes Filling The Air

Waiting for concreteness,
Desperate about permanence,
A wavering nature of life,
Paths waver, places waver,
Unequal movement with rapidity,
Changes with insanity,
Sweet changing to bitter,
Bitterness changing to neutrality,
Sadness amidst happiness,
Happiness happening sometime,
Sadness conquering every time,

The bitterness in kindness,
Everything present as an illusion,
The ill illusion everywhere,
Trueness hiding somewhere,
Permanence placed far away,
Reaching the destiny,
With concreteness on my way.

12. The Man

The wit and wittiness present,
A sufferer, suffering always,
Intellect and intelligence filling,
Toiled and toiling always,
Powerful presence at some place,
Overpowered in some way,
You are a providing provider,
Ugly ugliness seen earlier,
Gentleness accompanied with it,
Handsome and manly you are,
Manliness upon maturity visible,

Saintly or priestly are you becoming?
Or just simplicity with traditions,
Traditions seems to make a priest,
But not a high priest nor a saint,
A conservative conserving my family,
Traditions and my race,
With my community on my face,
A powerful conservative,
Crafted with gentleness.

13. The Moonlight

Light of dimness and whiteness,
Amidst the dark sea hanging,
Dot-sized lamp from faraway,
Huge and heaviness felt in you,
Nightmares and dreams coming,
Barks and howling tuned inside,
Stars accompany thee in plentitude,
Horror and calmness both surrounding,
Comfort and coldness for some,
Freezing chillness for some.

14. Rich Blackness

The deepness with darkness,
Deep seas and oceans,
Dark and black all around,
Treasures are found deep,
Hiding inside, richness hidden,
Treasures are always hidden,
Overcoming darkness all the way,
To conquer the richness,
The blackness is rich,
A richness in blackness.

15. Abandoned Past

A haunted place of memories,
Haunting memories of past,
Past passing by, to pass out,
The death of the past is final.
Living past with sweet memories,
But worries conquering the sweetness,
Cruelty making it to abandon all,
Past with sweetness is abandoned,
The past with cruelty holding along.

16. Creeping Creepiness

Darkness dark enough,
Creepiness creepy enough,
The movements of suddenness,
Life with fallenness and brokenness,
Dark thoughts during the dark time,
Confusions during the day time,
Gloominess gloomfully filling in,
Darkness blooming and coming in,
A small movement is scary,
Moving with weariness, so weary.

17. A Non-Living Companion

I can carry you on my back,
You help me carry the best,
A speechless and noiseless thing,
But you contain many things,
I like to lay you on the table,
Your companionship is needed,
You sit by my side, wherever I go,
I can buy you, mend you and sustain you,
You sustain what I carry in you,
Bearing the bearable quantity,

You are a non-living entity.

18. Harmless Thing

You do not demand,
Nor you command,
You cause no harm,
No physical nor emotional harm,
I need you by my side,
You carry what I need,
No voice to create noise,
You do not want anything,
You serve me with nothing less,
A quality of harmlessness,
I prefer you always,
Over a human companionship.

19. Hot And Damp

Under the presence of fire,
The ball of gases hanging higher,
Ozone protecting and comforting,
Ozone protecting every zone,
Many trials for the protector,
We are tending towards the destroyer,
The protected under protection,
But the protector suffering,
Protector is diminishing,
Diminishes by our comforts,

A hole is drilled unto it,
Draining the protection we get,
We tend towards the destruction,
The protector perishes and we perish,
A path of self-destruction.

20. The Piercing Pain

Edible becoming inedible,
Multiple needles piercing inside,
My skin is sensitized for pain,
Loss of appetite and no gain,
Skinny skin covering the top,
Discomfort conquering now,
Unable to rise up but falling down,
Delicious meal becoming plain,
The taste buds shutting down,
Smells to bring the river out,

But unable to crush and taste,
All the sweetness going to waste.

21. Calls Unheard

Sounds and noises surrounding,
Small voices revolving around,
Crowds might make noises,
Multiple voices overlapping,
Voices are heard calling,
Ignorable and unignorably heard,
Deafness turning to reality,
Ignoring the calls of divine being,
Calling followed by falling,
A fall never heard and unheard,
When a call becomes unheard.

22. Thorns Of Life

Darkness captured by sight,
Fearful, frightening and tiresome,
No space for light to fall on my sight,
Infections, venom and poison,
Stings, scratches and stabs,
Bleeding, fractured and breathless,
A living entity lying down lifeless,
Recovery, recharge and rest,
Denied for this soul forever,
To depart peacefully and rest.

23. Caught The Sight

Brightness and lightness,
The nature's light falling,
Nature calling the man,
Beauty of the creation,
The created inside the creation,
Creator above everything,
The lush green fields,
Windmills rotating,
Rotating rotations going,
Nature consuming my sight,
Blueness of the sky,
The big blue sea, so vast,

One needs a pause to view all,
A bright and pleasant sight of all.

24. Diseased Opinion

Rumors mourning everywhere,
Judgements blowing somewhere,
First sight of anything is concrete,
Human nature visible very discrete,
Facts driven opinions are forming,
Ruinsome people claiming,
The evilness always blaming,
Innate understanding under threats,
Opinions contaminated by some,
Disease spreading inside the mind,
Thoughts and actions changing,
Illness shaping the mind,

A diseased opinion forming,
Remedy of the innateness fighting,
Anti-thought factors coming,
Conflicts arising in the mind,
True premise winning and controlling,
The diseased mind with ill thoughts,
Diminishing and dulling,
Healthy mind with pure thoughts,
Innate victory controlling.

25. Healing Wounds

Slippery and falling nature,
Tripped and cracking stones,
Breaking my bones all alone,
Weariness and dullness,
No light for brightness,
All tied up by a bonding,
A whiteness tying many,
Broken bonds mended,
My deep wounds are browning,
Scars are coming, stars are fading,
Fading scars come upon me,
Healing wounds are steady,

My soul is healing my wounds.

26. Exceeding Dislike

Seeds of dislike sown in fertile grounds,
Roots catching hold and firm they are,
More seeds produced to get away,
Trees with many branches grown,
Fruits produced and falling down,
Inedible and saltiness filling it,
Dislike for sweets and sugars around,
Salt preferred over sweetness when needed,
Bitterness filling the ground and all around,
Boundaries formed and rejection in it's highest,
Innocence in it's lowest and forever absent,
Acknowledgement terminated to stop,

Ignorance becomes the key to unlock,
Unleashing my interests over a dislikable present,
Waiting for time to pass on, for future to come,
Growing dislike among the present time,
Rooting out the present life to enter a happy future.

27. Never Ending

Time moving away, a pleasant, present time,
Happiness moving away like the sunlight,
Sweetness moving apart like the moonlight,
Success departing away like a breeze,
Everything imparting ease and comfort,
Moving away all the ground for peace.
Time in slowness, ticking each second,
The worst of times seems so long to pass away,
Sadness standing like the immovable skies,
Bitterness staying like a still vast ocean,
Failures caged like a mad dog's madness,
Anything imparting dis-ease and irritation,

Staying close by, and brokenness growing within.

28. Edible Chemicals

Multiple colours available,
Pure whiteness and bitterness,
Capsulated capsules containing it,
White dust with heavy bitterness,
Dullness with sweetness for cure,
Illness demanding sharp needles,
Stopping the contamination,
Liquids of redness with purity,
Sweet syrups and white spheres,
Duration controlling the bitterness,
Termination attained by the cure.

29. Congested Spaces

Wooden blocks arranged,
Nailed and painted for beauty,
Small pieces with sponges embedded,
Glass screwed with the steel rods,
Papers and covers all lying around,
Material acquisition is unstoppable,
Libraries filling up, tables piled up,
Cupboards stuffed up with stuffs,
No place to move around,
An irritable congestion all around.

30. Cracks And Peels

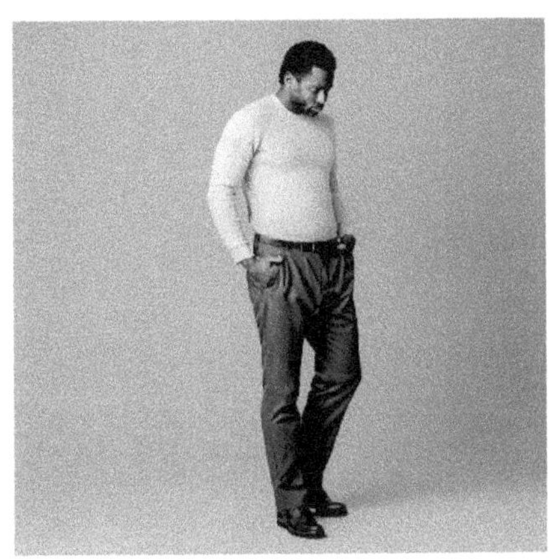

Walking all around,
Foot swelled up with saltiness,
Wet foot covering all over,
Peeling off my toes,
Protective covering torn apart,
Burning and itching prevailing,
Wounded stays my foot,
Bleeding is impossible,
Rusted with a pile of dust,
Oiled up, to mend it up.

31. Broken Apart

Rusting bridges, narrow ridges,
Powdered with rust and dust,
Rust holding on for years,
Breaking with cracks each year,
Murmurs becoming great roars,
Silence becoming ever-absent,
Slippery and flexible to inflexible,
Breaking rather than bending,
Tolerance is hidden forever,
Burning with sheer coldness,
Rusted due to an ever-present dampness.

32. Worthless Entity

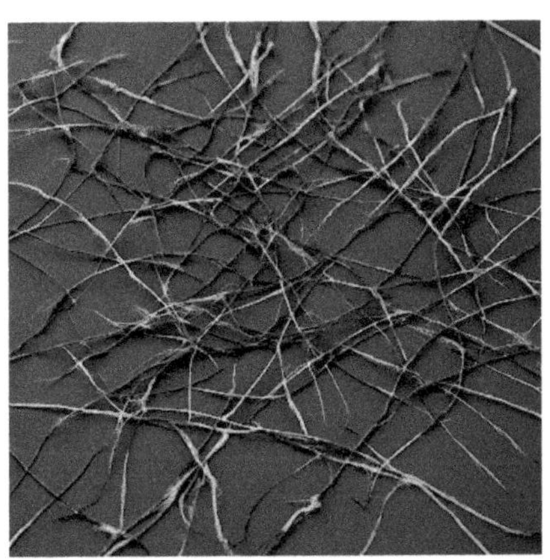

Printed papers and a weird smell,
Silvers and gold, not so bold,
Freedom becoming shinning gold,
Ornaments and fancies with fakeness,
Inequality in wealth and joy,
Living entity is not a toy,
Artificiality fading away,
Nature taking it's way,
Words becoming mere sounds,
No more are we bound.

33. The Medicine

Wavering nature is the purest,
Pleasant wetness surrounding all around,
Dryness to make way for the ground,
Crowded and organized everywhere,
Richness and nobility in the blood,
Primitive richness and tradition is here.

34. Like A Fine Wine

The book of life unlocking the mystery,
Pages written down creating the history,
Sweetness and plump at the tree,
The stages move up as one, two and three,
First stage of growth done internally,
Growing and ripening insanity,
The glowing wondrous maturity,
Child-like and innocent being,
Hanging on the tree growing,
Second stage of growth done externally,
Less hairy and shaggy with purity,
Brokenness in innocence and child,

The child within is vanishing,
A man is born within and beyond,
The final step is reached within,
Hairy and shaggy with wild eyes,
The chapters moving to a climax,
History turning into a mystery,
Gentlemanly and wildness intersecting,
Primitiveness of the land and nativity,
Nativity and the native-land recovering,
The bearded wildness causing chillness,
Like a fine wine, I am growing.

35. Living The Future

Waves of passion in the ocean,

Vastness in space and time,

A giant growing inside the space,

Thoughts and ideas placed inside,

Dumped and packed tightly to bear,

Thinking becoming overthinking,

Optimism changing to pessimism,

Calmness changing to arrogance,

Losing the present life of happiness,

Past mistakes taking over the present,

Mistakes leading to a dead end,

The misery of confusions in a student,

Mistakes repeating itself like a history,
Planning the future and pausing the present.

36. Service And Serving

From the bottom of the heart,
The roots are rooted, deep inside,
Kindness and politeness,
Growing and reaching everywhere,
The shoots spread apart and away,
A body paving every way,
Tips reaching the extreme ends,
Heart touching all the limbs,
Touched the mind and brain,
Involuntary actions of kindness,
Limbs and mind moving swiftly,
Thoughts rolling briskly.

37. Impression Or Judgement

The first sight of unhealthiness,
Thoughts of rottenness and sickness,
Involuntariness in the mind and heart,
Thoughts reverberating on it's own,
Innate thinking and analysis going,
My sight and thinking are paralyzed,
Goodness and evilness being balanced.
The voluntary thoughts and sight,
Thoughts of elegance and arrogance,
Voluntary movement in the mind and heart,
Thinking deeply for thoughts to come out,
Biased thinking and a wavering premise,

Factors determining the outcome,
A judgement without innateness and a premise.

38. Passive Strength

Manuscripts of the past,

Browning and yellowing down,

Reverberated from the heart, deep down,

Eyes rolling and capturing all,

Passiveness making a call,

Words joined, making a simple gown,

Whiteness and purity in simplicity,

Heaviness in heavenly words written,

Lightness in lips and heart in return,

Branches growing deep inside,

Strong natured, and a song growing,

Versified verses written long back,

The tree of mind is browning within,
Fruits of wisdom and words given out,
Freely given but none to receive,
Plentitude and riches to deceive.

39. Primitive Elegance

Present and pastness as a mixture,
Forming a fine and beautiful texture,
An attire of formalness and formality,
Tinted with a partial beast and a man,
Inked and pierced with silver and iron,
Rings of silver and gold for the man,
Black, brown and greyness dominating,
Hairy and bulky with a control to make,
Dusky, dark and roughness of the man,
Uncontrolled, hairy and shaggy,
Makes up a poor stray doggy,
Controlled intermingling is awesome,

Elegance in primitivity is fearsome.

40. The Touch Screen

Emitter of light and radiations,
Irritating and pricking sensations,
World moving faster and faster,
Connections growing larger and larger,
Screen with a variety of purpose,
Proteins making up the lens is weakened,
Optics creating a multiple vision,
Visions of blurriness and weakness,
A four-eyed vision is witnessed,
Addictions getting injected into the limbs,
Scrolling past and eyes rolling over,
The migraine makes the game over.

41. Lights Off

Thunderstorms and wetness prevailing,
Bolts of flashes from the sky coming,
Bursts and cuts and there comes the power cut,
Electrons moving into each house being stopped,
The pause made as an action of protection,
Termination of the misery by fire is done,
Short-circuiting may tend a short human life,
Vision of television flickering and flashing out,
Lights popping on and shutting off,
Darkness surrounding every corner of the house,
Dark and darkened with fear of the dark night,
Light amidst the darkness is flashing back again.

42. The Adulthood

Musicality of the life stopping,
Carelessness and gentleness fading,
Dependence changing to independence,
Happiness and politeness losing their essence,
An ever chattering noise box,
Turning into an air of silence,
Cunning and swift as a fox,
The seed turned into a fruit,
The fruit to be harvested,
Ripened ones already in the basket,
Silence is valued and preserved,
Earthly life strongly observed,

Morality and ethics strictly conserved,
Maturity is gifted and rightly deserved,
Bearded with passion and desire,
Difficulties of the past,
The frightening nature ever lost,
Evilness and rottenness of the world,
Never will it touch the heart and mind,
Materialistic pleasures are diminished,
Achievements are now cherished,
Gifts of artificiality rejected,
A briefcase of knowledge is collected,
Approachable for kindness,
But now protected by roughness,
A mature roughness present forever.

43. Diminishing Physicality

Words written with the ink,
The inked words and works,
Becoming typed words,
Books of paper and pages,
Diminishing into the screens,
Felt the words in my hands,
No essence, now present in them.
Captured moments of the past,
Instruments of captures lost,
Handy are the electronics becoming,
Every second being captured,
The essence of waiting is lost,

Patience and values of many lost,
The physicality at the verge of extinction,
A diminishing physicality in progress.

44. Repetitions Repeating

Chains of repetition happening,
The cycles of events in the play of life,
Disasters repeating and causing distractions,
Tragedies and miseries paving way for sadness,
Actions and staleness repeating,
A repetition in the life process and progress,
Cycles of heat and anger revolving,
Revolutions and coldness in war continuing,
Repetitions rotating all around renewing,
Words and letters repeating itself,
Sensical or non-sensical sometimes,
Ideas and thoughts renewed and repeated,

Discoveries and inventions, a modification,
Newness becoming an ever repeating entity.

45. Strength And Shield

Courage raging like a fire,
The present age of desire,
Changes repelled earlier,
Accepting to rebel and change,
The fashion of passion requires,
Changes in physicality for strength,
A partial beast to shield,
Masculine power under use,
Opposite opposing to misuse,
The child is dead long back,
A man is made and living somewhere.

46. Native Land

The blood connects with the air,
Foot merging with the soil and found nowhere,
Nature connecting with the nature,
Contamination draining away,
From the flesh, blood and soul,
A clarity given to the mind and soul,
In a simple and primitive nature,
Freshness ruling everywhere,
Blackness no more in the air,
Madness terminated from the head,
Health increasing in manifold,
Simplicity making a healthy being.

47. Mixture

An equal composition combining,
Darkness and fairness together,
Every colours and shapes forming,
Each one in it's own and one way,
Rocks and sands as a mixture,
Brown and roughness in texture,
Saltiness and neutrality together,
Seas and oceans with no boundaries,
A composed and an uncomposed mixture,
The world in it's own texture.

48. Nature's Colours

Energy giving colours of the world,
My heart starts pumping more blood,
Earthly colours of brown, blue and green,
The soil spread all around in a dream,
Blue sky of cooling quality, a cool entity,
Green life, giving the air, it gently cares,
Clothed in the colours of the earth,
The brown and khaki of masculinity,
Blueness coming with neutrality,
A green mother earth for the femininity,
Colours to stop the human insanity,
And forever maintaining the purity.

49. Like A Coin

Head or the tail, matters a lot,
The two extreme ends of a being,
Baby and a child at one side,
The innocence and kindness,
Forming the boundaries for some,
Selective behaviour given to some,
Sociable and calmness comes,
The coin is tossed to see the next one,
A roughness with the gruffness,
Toughness in it's highest point,
A man and a beast is present,
Forming boundaries for the death,

A dead relation of toxicity,
Terminated by the selectiveness.

50. The Finish Line

Accomplished accomplishments raining,
The words and letters brought the wetness all around,
First day of the three verses, spreading like a river,
The daily verses, some of innocence and others of curses,
The toil written down by the dust of the soil,
Faculty of mind, heart and body in it's finest,
The first print of the fifty verses and curses,
Happiness accompanied by a disappointment,
None can stop the verses and curses,
Verses intensified to the highest and lowest,
The second papers of fifty verses fired out,
The darkness overtaking all over the verses,

A marathon of the next hundred verses going,
The day it is over, the finish line is reached,
From poetry and poems, everything came out,
Hidden gems of the past, present and future,
These two hundred verses, speaking to some,
The movement towards the next journey,
Finally, the prosaic journey had begun.

I Admire You: A Self-admiration Of My Inner Feelings

I Admire You is a collection of poetry which deals with feelings and emotions that reach the extremities. A life which gives you a spoonful of all the feelings in every stage of growing up is described. The feelings and emotions are weaved using words to create this collection of poetry. The title is given due to the self-admiration of my inner feelings.

'Very nice, practical and motivating. Need to read once daily...'

- Regular reader of 'Anglistik with Abraham'

Publisher: BookLeaf Publishing, Srinagar

ISBN: 9789358316506

Published on: November 13, 2023

• 80 •

Loud Inner Voice: Multiple Voices Ringing Inside

Loud Inner Voice is a collection of 50 poems that views the everyday life in a scrutinized manner. The poems are written from the varoius thoughts that rings in my mind to create a variety of voices.

Publisher: Notion Press, Chennai

ISBN: 9798893223248

Published on: March 7, 2024

Sweetness In Nostalgia: Cherishing The Past And Living The Present

Sweetness In Nostalgia is a collection of 50 poems which talks about finding comfort from the sweet memories of the past when the present times are filled with bitterness. The poems oscillate from bitterness to sweetness and then ends with a note of neutrality and acceptance.

Publisher: Notion Press, Chennai

ISBN: 9798894467351 (Paperback)

ISBN: 9798894467368 (Hardcover)

Published on: June 17, 2024

www.ingramcontent.com/pod-product-compliance
Lightning Source LLC
Chambersburg PA
CBHW040824120726

48005CB00012B/1501